# Night Boat to Ninevah

Kathy MacGloin

BookLeaf Publishing

India | USA | UK

Presentation by *BookLeaf Publishing*

Web: www.bookleafpub.com

E-mail: info@bookleafpub.com

ISBN: 9789360949594

First edition 2024

# The Call

What were you at, Jonah, when you heard
the voice of God?  Were you engaging
in the doldrums?  That numbing weight
that smothers some, but not enough, the
cricket-call
of conscience.  In the beginning was
the Word,
and the Word told you to get up.

Get up and go to Ninevah.  How
did it feel, Jonah, to get that call?
To hear the whispered certainty beyond
the storms of daily life.  That still small voice
of calm.  I'm asking, Jonah, because I am afraid
that I already know, or can imagine
that it swam up within you, a great
eel of a thought, swelling your chest
and brushing past your heart, lifting,
sinking, pushing, pressing it,
closer to your breastbone, and living on your
breath.

Get up. Get thee to Ninevah.  Did you balk?
Jonah?  Did you
fear madness, or crave comfort?  I do

believe, I know, that I would think
of these; of ease and how preferable it would be
to please myself, and others, had I received
a missive call.  How it would gall me to
rale against the rock of prestige, whilst anchoring
each carabiner of my day into the sturdy
face it provides.  Get up.  Would I

respond to such a rousing cry?  Disguised
within the humming tinnitus, the strumming stridulations
of an ingloriously, unglamorous weight
upon my shoulder.

# Jonah answers God

I have zeal for your service.  I've that measured,
steady kind that lends itself to mission, where
mission
is inclined to be at least a little sweetened with
that balm
of security.  I have prayed.  I don't want
accolade but freedom
from concern.  Grant me mission, God in
Heaven.  Just not this one.

I do not ask for much.  Just the bracing support
of familiarity.
The touch of structure, habit, a safe place, while
I'm about your business.
I know that in my weakness glow the embers of
your grace,
and deep within, where stillness burns, I wonder
what you could
accomplish through me.  God all knowing, you
can send me.  Anywhere but there.

Were I to stride up to the gates, and stand beside
the stone lamassus
I'd not inspire anything.  I'd not make these
stone bulls tremble, drifting

gypsum from their wings.  I'd be a gnat amidst
their greatness.  Mighty
God, they would crush me.  Let destruction be
their fate, then.
Let me not be called a "madman" by bringing
truth into this city.
Why show pagans any pity.  Why be so
ubiquitous with mercy?

Would you let them mock me?  Would you let
me
hand myself over to a crowd quite so unworthy?
Would you
let them strip and bind me, let them beat and
undermine me?
If I went, declaring repentence, I would die
amidst these people.
At their hand.  And in their land.  This is hard.
And I must
struggle from the ring of your embrace, like a
child.  I must
run from You, my God.  I am fugitive from
grace.

# Sights on Tarshish

I'll plumb for Malaga,
its baking stones, and sardine smells
and long-haired, almond-eyed, señoritas.

I'll stare, eyes glazed, into the half-distance,
through air made molten by heat, set alight
by the incessant crackling stick-legs of cicadas.

I'll bear the trickling spindles of sweat
tearing down the gutter of my spine and deep
in my ungirded loins, the seep of salt.

Yes, I'll skulk aboard a ship, and in shadows,
steal
away from zealous trips.  I'll face, in flight, the
sight
of straights that make the mirage fate of castles
in the air

upended.

# At Joppa

I haunt this harbour. All others are all about
their business in this salt-fringed Philistine town.
I am
shrouded by the bugle bartering of tradesmen,
the rousing reveille and keening cry of the sea
birds.

The unseen
clinging barnacles of conscience are borne
by me as pockmarks.  Where chatter stops
against my skin
I consider these salt-crustings of my soul
I whisper, Jonah: the unworthy.
The unclean.  Unanswered
mission stowed in the depth of me
will have to act as ballast.  I'll leave

Joppa.  Your name echoes
the rolling slap of sea against the belly of the
boats.
Joppa.  The rocking, teasing
might of swell, feigning tameness as it nuzzles
the dock.
Joppa. Joppa. Joppa.

Ah Joppa, your mouth open to drink the sea.
Once
was delivered to you the cedars
of Lebanon, the struts for Solomon's temple.
Now, I sit upon your lip like a splinter to be spat
out.

# The Bosun thinks on Jonah

Still, my wee boat;
it's a strange man sleeps like the dead
in the face of rough weather.

He'd the look of fear
of shadows, of one who'd run from something
pinned to his own back.

And now he sleeps like a dead weight,
like a stone in the hold, sunk
in the bulge of your belly.

Haunted, I'd say.
Pitch and toss, such is life! maybe
love, loss, or wife, ghosts his eyes.

# The Captain thinks on Jonah

This man would hide his hunted look.
But see, small muscles dart and flick about his
face
like small fish, twitching at the water's surface.

And look, sweat shines in the dim light,
salty rain across his brow; a briny dew lines his
lip
He drinks of it, when he thinks I see not.

He's paid his passage before the trip,
swift slip of silver too readily given
Sin that pays its way travels freely

See how he burns to leave!
And he would soothe the simmering
that won't be cooled by the entire ocean's gift.

No peace.  His fingers tremble;
they show the zephyr fringes of the storm
that rips between the sail-strung lungs within

# The First Watch thinks on Jonah

By Charybdis, Captain, I'd not take that man
as crew or as freight.  Unless it's to calm,
As bait, the black heart of Scylla, I'd not let him
cast
his shadow, or sorrow, or step treacherous sole

on our ship.  By mermaids and fish-tailed
frights,
tentacled, barnacled, kelp-clad and coral-clung
coracles,
Captain,

My Captain, you've marked us
as fodder for fishes.  As flotsam and jetsam
for strewing from ships wrecked, for spewing
from maelstroms.

# Second Watch thinks on Jonah

Where was the farewell?

The tear-rinsed, slender-armed
grappling, that clings on the neck until prised
away?  Where was the hour-glass
figure of woman?  Hip strut to bear
an unblinking babe?  Where
was the baggage? The world
in a bindle
wrapped
in a promise.

I promise
this man is a curse and is chaos.

# The Crew wake Jonah.

12

Awake now, and get up.  Unburden
yourself and us with your confession.
What have you done?  What sorrow
you bring as baggage on this ship.
Was it albatross and anchor that you stowed?
Draw your lot, salted by the sea's hungry breath
look back, and see the fruit of your refusal.

# Jonah responds

I am fugitive from that which cannot be fled.
I run from the air I breathe.
I flee from the arms that, even now, caress
my skin.  I quell the blood that pumps within.
The dry land, the empty void.  These were not vacant
of Him who wrests the water into churning.
I suffocate with sorrow since
I run from the very act of Being.

# The Crew Pray

The mast swings as pendulum
marking the passing of our indecision.
We are the drowned moments before the
drowning

The wind beats a death march on the strung
sails:
a warning.  Our rowing, mere token.  The ocean
is open to filling our sponge-lungs with
salt-water
hushing with stillness our hearts' merry
drumming.

Jonah, you hoisted the mainsail of chaos.
God forgive us, we know not what You do.
Jonah, we throw you over
as anchor in your Beloved's storm.

# The Storm is Calmed

The sea enveloped Jonah,
the man, the curse, the prophet
it closed behind him, and the water's surface
became as glass.  The silvery contour of the
moon's edges
reformed, no longer storm-shattered into
crystals.
And each man on board, as though with
hollowed bones,
and brittle mind, kept a fragile, watchful,
silence.  Until
the more practical of them hoisted once again
and set a course to Tarshish.

# Drowning

I am crowned by seaweed, robed in ocean up to
my neck.
the weight of this garment of sea overwhelms
me
I have run from grace to death.  I have swum
as far as I can swim.  Fingers of water entwine
and entangle
and my eyes are covered in brine, only some of
which
is of my own making.  This darkness, I know to
be mine.

# God's haiku

My love, for your sake
I swallow in to stillness
your heart's disquiet

# Swallowed

Swallowed into such depths, I think on choices:
There exists one where You hand me grace and I
accept.

This choice gets up immediately.  Responds,
and is not caged by fear, like this whale's ribcage
holds me here.

You do not force, but ask.  A gentle invitation, a
still
small voice of calm.  The first choice sings a
"Fiat" and life begins.

The first choice walks into uncertainty with trust
in nothing other than Your sustaining it.  It is
alive

with vigour, with trial and error strung.  And joy
whether battle lost or battle won.  It holds man's
victory

as none.  The first choice is united, heart and
soul.
It is whole, and knows that it is loved.  It sings at
life.

The other choice refuses grace.  When weakness
overcomes my fickle heart.  When I rely upon
the meat

and bones of my own body.  Dust from ages past
and that will pass.  Like leaning on ashes for
support

and drowning in a burnt out fire.  The second
choice
hushes all the inner hopes.  The truth of who I
am is muffled.

It talks of failure, trials and suffering as though
these are final things;
offers comfort short-lived - a single breeze on
breathless seas.

Are there depths You do not know?  I am
brought as low
as I can bear.  Encased in shadows, I call.
You come and meet me there
and show me all the wounds of life.  And sit a
while.
And hold the aching bones that tried to run from
You.
And take my second choice, and in Your loving
alchemy

You wash and make all things new.  Even knowledge
of my weakness becomes a way of loving You.
If I call out from the depths of my sorrow, or shame
as heavy as leviathan, You listen and convert
this time of waiting, this dark encasing
to chrysalis and transformation.

# Night boat to Nineveh

Three days, three nights, senses stilled.
Entombed
in calm; enshrined in enforced rest.  Deep cries
unto deep, and Jonah re-receives himself;
healing comes
with mission though.  Get up again.  And again
and again
and an ocean's breadth is nothing.  Leviathan
movements
part the waves, and, like another birth
out of water comes Jonah, to pick up
his mission of metanoia.

# Sackcloth and Ashes

The gnat flew to the lamassus and whispered in
the beasts' ear
Look beyond - widen your sights - fold your
wings away
and lie down in your gypsum dust.
And the beasts bent low, and hid their faces, for
they had seen
their own reflections, so small, they could fit in a
gnat's eye.

The sea-spewed man, walked through the city
and his feet left pools behind.  And in these
pools the King
and people of the city looked and found that they
were called
to look beyond a muddied reflection of who they
were and are
and would be to come.  They put on sackcloth
and shone.

# Bitter Gourd

Only sun and moon passed over.
Jonah watched, but no flood,
no wave of destruction came.

Oh storm-strung Jonah: are you hero
with a promise kept, or madman
with an empty threat?

Salty Jonah.  He'd rather die than seem the fool.
His burning will to be admired has dried away
the cloak of learning from the sea.

"Are you right?" said God "to be angry?".

In peace, in absence of destruction, in silence,
sullen Jonah fell again to self-
imposed solitude and housed himself in
shadows.

He lay beneath the bulbous, hanging weights
of gourds; his roof - verdant succulence; his
window
ripe for Nineveh's fall. Until a worm,

infesting pleasures withered all.  So bitter

was the prophet then! Bitter Jonah, God makes
and takes.  And yet you claim some portion.

But God will save that city full of men.